test pattern

Cedar Waxwing

PLATE 1

Cedar Waxwing

PLATE 1

Yellow-eyed Junco

test pattern

PLATE 2

Yellow-eyed Junco

test pattern

PLATE 2

test pattern

Downny Woodpecker

test pattern

Allen's Hummingbird

PLATE 3

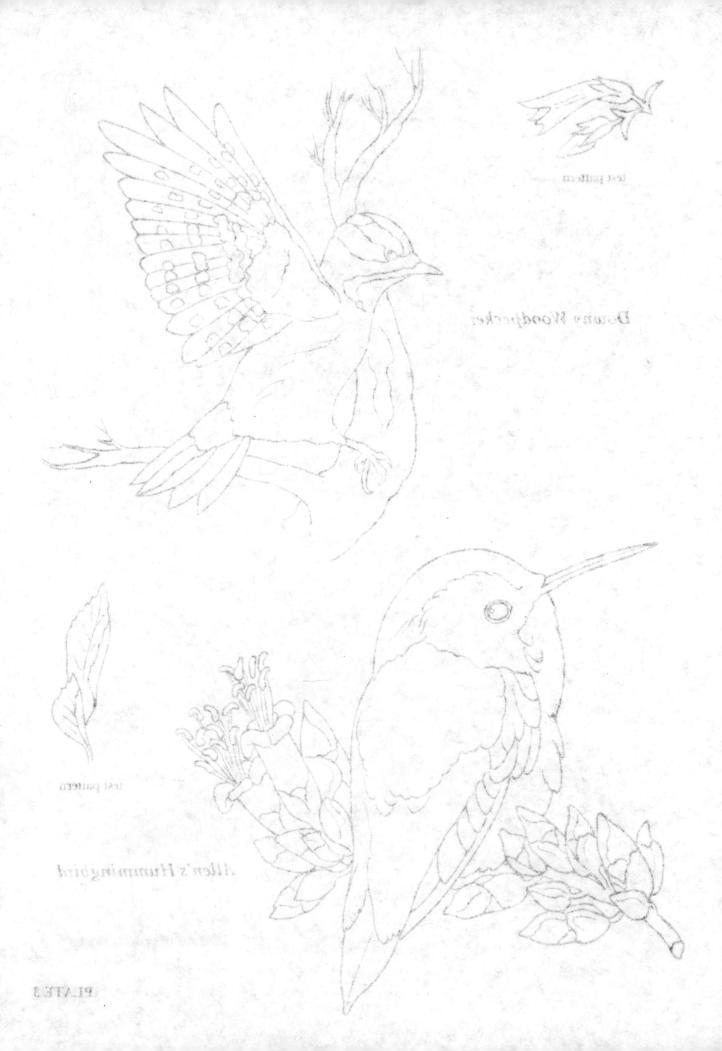

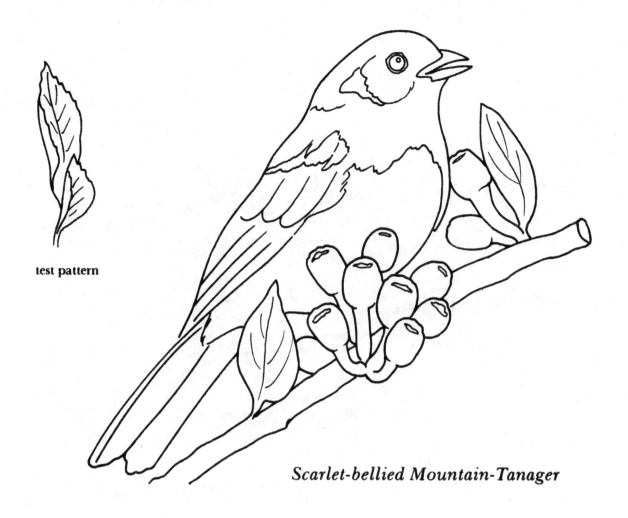

test pattern

Scarlet-bellied Mountain-Tanager

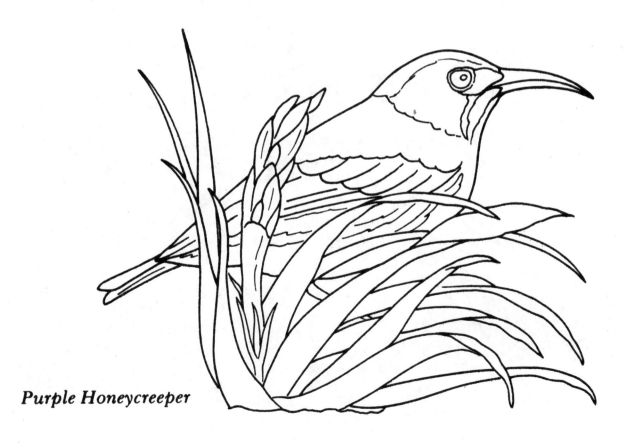

Purple Honeycreeper

PLATE 4

test pattern

Scarlet-bellied Mountain-Tanager

Purple Honeycreeper

PLATE 1

Long-tailed Antbird

test pattern

Yellow-billed Jacamar

PLATE 5

Long-tailed Aubbird

test pattern

Yellow-billed Jacamar

PLATE 5

Bee Eaters

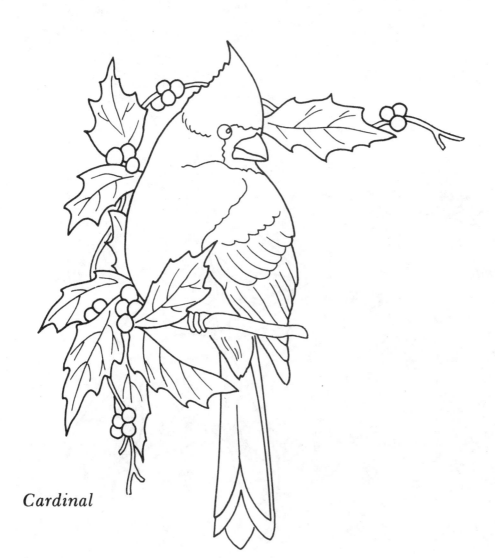

Cardinal

Mallards

PLATE 6

Bee Eaters

Mallards

Cardinal

PLATE 6

test pattern

Red-breasted Nuthatch

Mountain Chickadee

PLATE 7

Red-breasted Nuthatch

Mountain Chickadee

PLATE 7

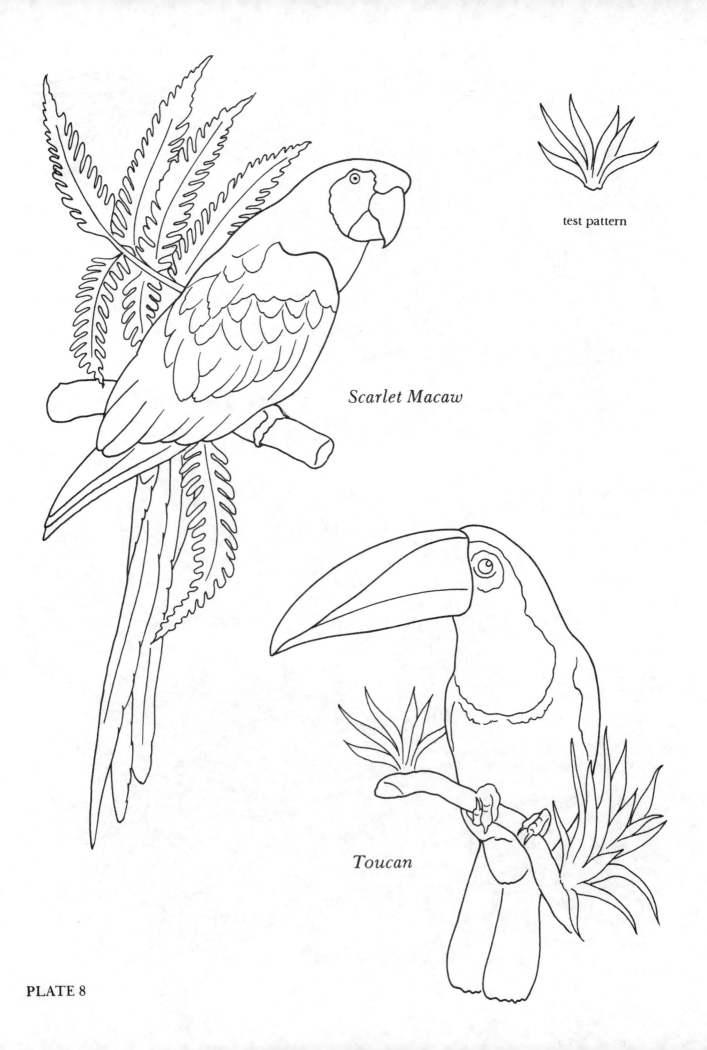

test pattern

Scarlet Macaw

Toucan

PLATE 8

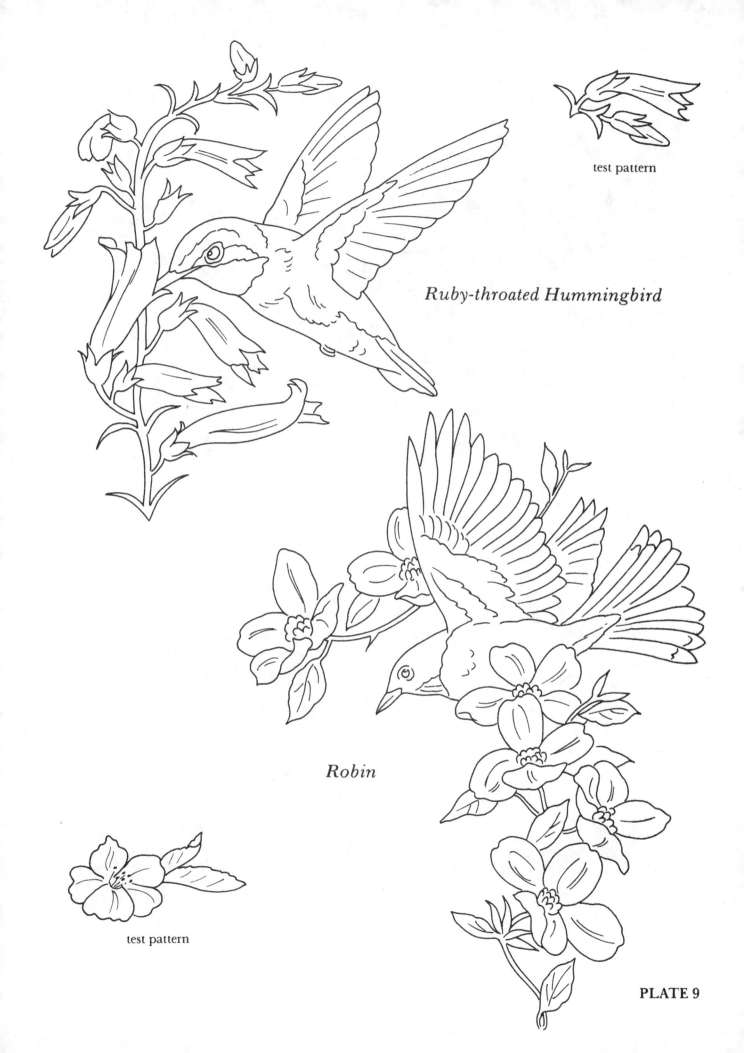

Ruby-throated Hummingbird

test pattern

Robin

test pattern

PLATE 9

test pattern

test pattern

Penguins

Eastern Phoebe

PLATE 10

Eastern Phoebe.

Penguins.

PLATE 10

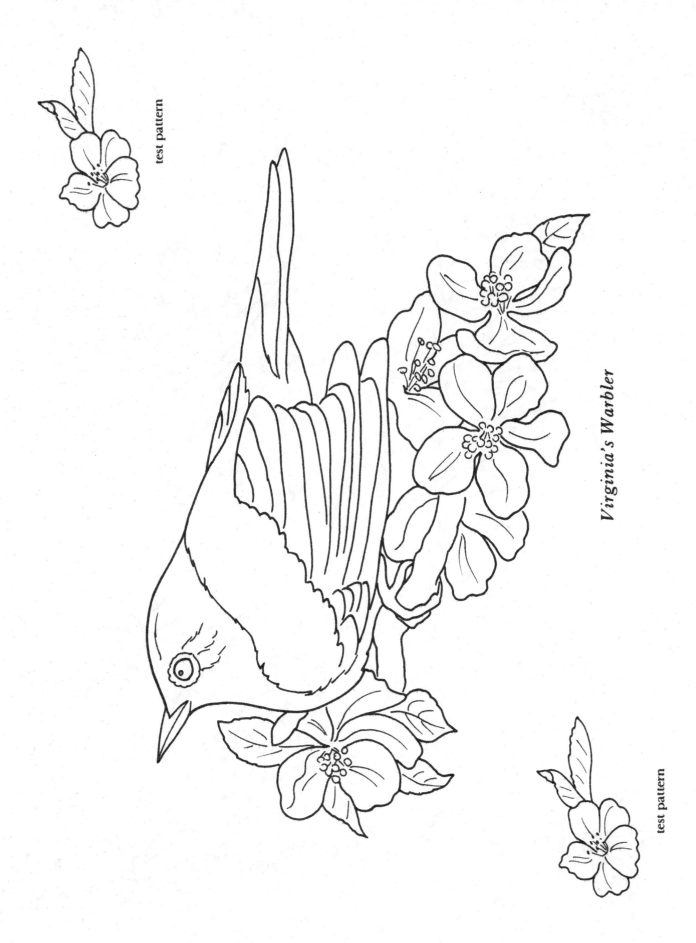

test pattern

Virginia's Warbler

test pattern

PLATE 11

PLATE 11

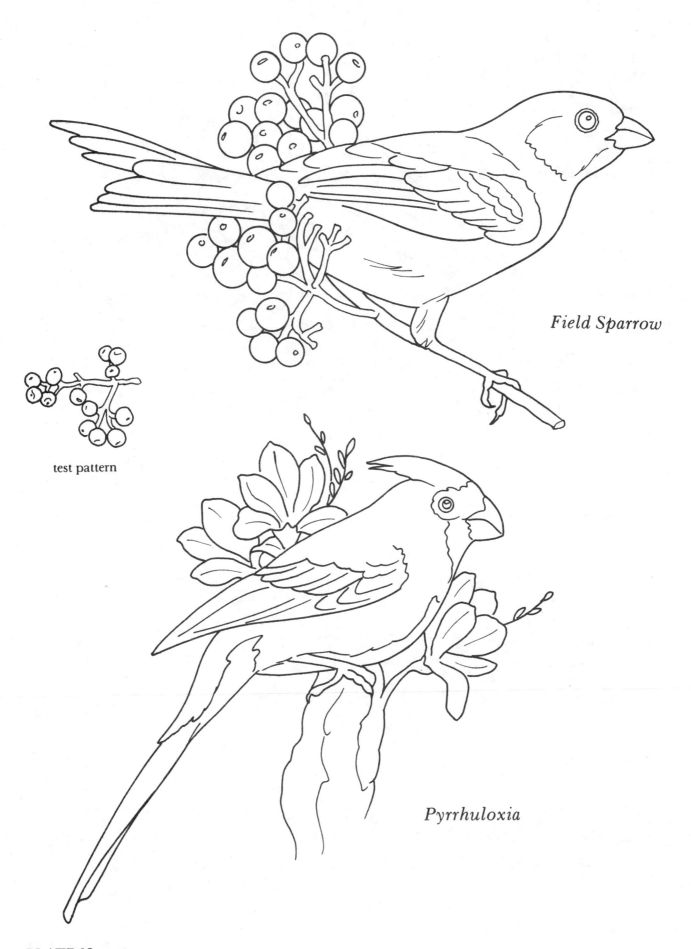

Field Sparrow

test pattern

Pyrrhuloxia

PLATE 12

test pattern

Red-faced Warbler

PLATE 13

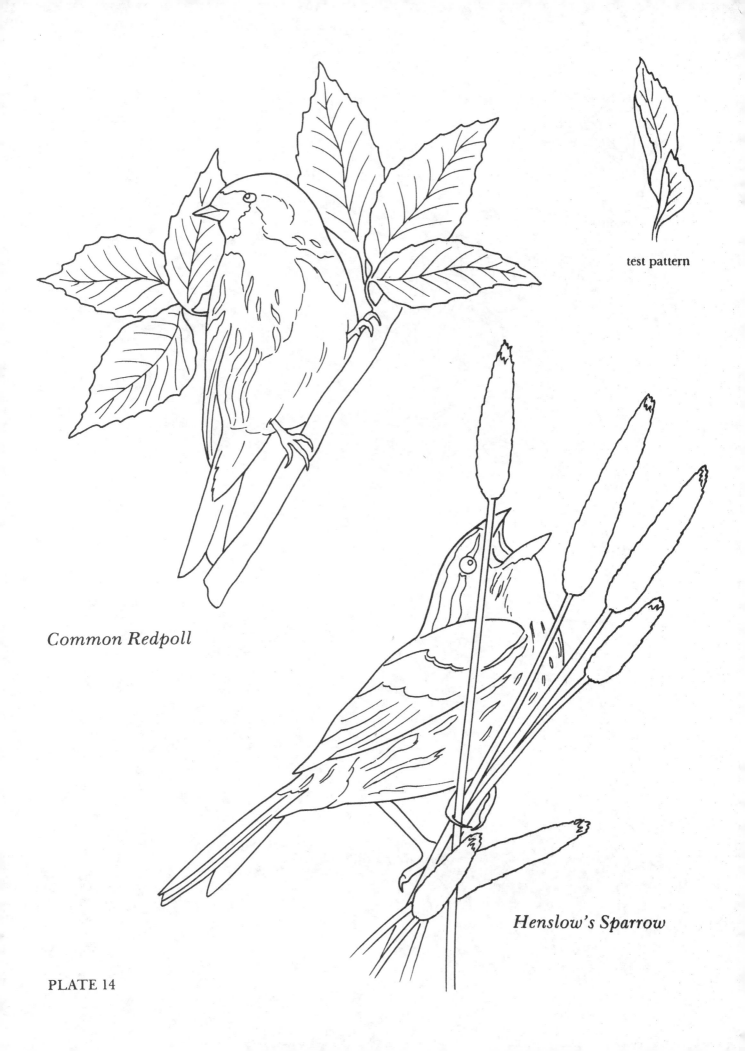

test pattern

Common Redpoll

Henslow's Sparrow

PLATE 14

test pattern

American Goldfinch

PLATE 15

Rose-breasted Grosbeak

test pattern

Indigo Flower-piercer

Hummingbirds

PLATE 16

Rose-breasted Grosbeak

test pattern

Hummingbirds

Indigo Flower-piercer

PLATE 16

Northern (Baltimore) Oriole

test pattern

Western Meadowlark

PLATE 17

Northern (Baltimore) Oriole

Western Meadowlark

PLATE 15

test pattern

Townsend's Warbler

PLATE 18

test pattern

Green Jay

Blue Jay

PLATE 19

test pattern

Green Jay

Blue Jay

PLATE 19

test pattern

House Sparrow

PLATE 20

House Sparrow

PLATE 40

test pattern

Eastern Wood Peewee

PLATE 21

Eastern Wood Pewee

PLATE 21

test pattern

Rosy-faced Lovebirds

PLATE 22

Rosy-faced Lovebirds

1st pattern

PLATE 22

test pattern

Barn Swallow

PLATE 23

test-pattern

Barn Swallow

PLATE 25

Great Blue Heron

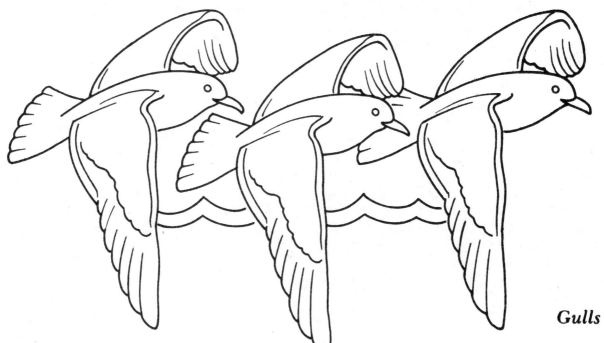

Gulls

PLATE 24

Great Blue Heron

Gulls

PLATE 24